The WORLD of INSECTS

INSECT HOMES

Bobbie Kalman & John Crossingham

Crabtree Publishing Company

www.crabtreebooks.com

Insect Homes

Created by Bobbie Kalman

Dedicated by John Crossingham
For Xander, my first nephew

Editor-in-Chief
Bobbie Kalman

Writing team
Bobbie Kalman
John Crossingham

Substantive editor
Kelley MacAulay

Project editor
Molly Aloian

Editors
Robin Johnson
Rebecca Sjonger
Kathryn Smithyman

Design
Margaret Amy Salter

Production coordinator
Heather Fitzpatrick

Photo research
Crystal Foxton

Consultant
Patricia Loesche, Ph.D., Animal Behavior Program,
Department of Psychology, University of Washington

Illustrations
Barbara Bedell: page 9
Katherine Kantor: page 24
Bonna Rouse: back cover, pages 5, 15, 18, 19, 28
Margaret Amy Salter: pages 20, 30-31
Tiffany Wybouw: page 16

Photographs
© Alexey Lisovoy. Image from BigStockPhoto.com: page 7 (top)
© Can Stock Photo Inc.: dwags: page 28
James Kamstra: pages 13 (right), 14, 16, 26
© Dwight Kuhn: pages 10, 11, 19, 25, 27
robertmccaw.com: pages 13 (left), 17 (bottom)
iStockphoto.com: AravindTeki: page 23; Rick Jones: page 29;
    Viktor Kitaykin: page 20; Chartchai Meesangnin: pages 22, 24;
    Greg Nicholas: page 7 (bottom); Jeffrey Zavitski: page 17 (top)
James H. Robinson/Photo Researchers, Inc.: page 12
Other images by Brand X Pictures, Corel, Digital Vision, and
    Otto Rogge Photography

Crabtree Publishing Company

www.crabtreebooks.com   1-800-387-7650

Cataloging-in-Publication Data
Kalman, Bobbie.
  Insect homes / Bobbie Kalman & John Crossingham.
    p. cm. -- (The world of insects series)
  Includes index.
  ISBN-13: 978-0-7787-2345-5 (rlb)
  ISBN-10: 0-7787-2345-3 (rlb)
  ISBN-13: 978-0-7787-2379-0 (pbk)
  ISBN-10: 0-7787-2379-8 (pbk)
  1. Insects--Habitations--Juvenile literature. I. Crossingham, John. II. Title.
  QL467.2.K359 2006
  595.7156'4--dc22
                                                              2005035798
                                                              LC

**Published in
the United States**
PMB16A
350 Fifth Ave.
Suite 3308
New York, NY
10118

**Published
in Canada**
616 Welland Ave.
St. Catharines, Ontario
Canada
L2M 5V6

**Published in the
United Kingdom**
White Cross Mills
High Town, Lancaster
LA1 4XS
United Kingdom

**Published
in Australia**
386 Mt. Alexander Rd.
Ascot Vale (Melbourne)
VIC 3032

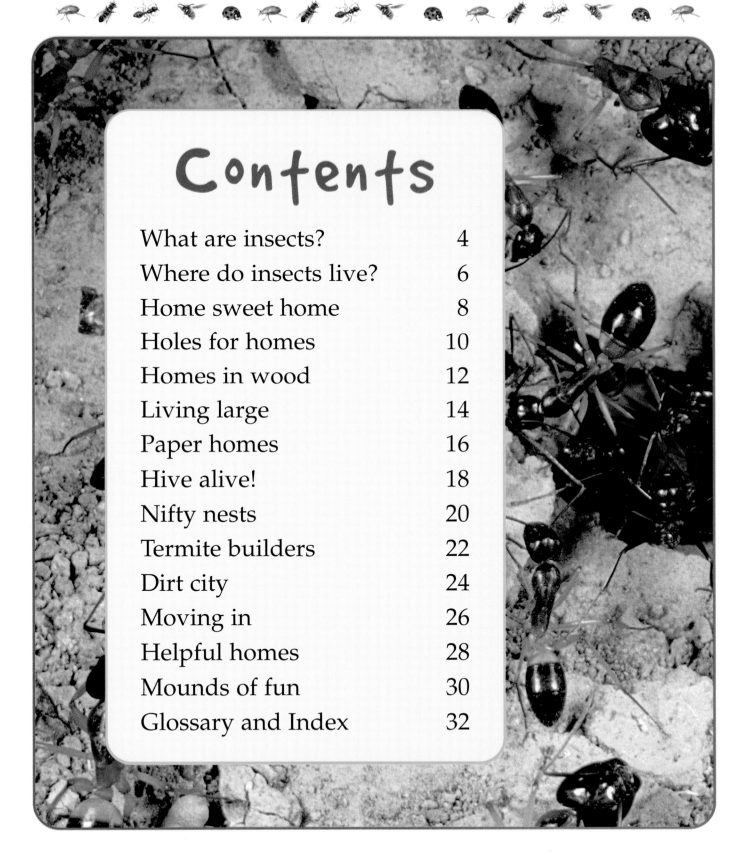

Contents

What are insects?

Insects are animals. They do not have **backbones**. A backbone is a group of bones in the middle of an animal's back. Animals that do not have backbones are called **invertebrates**.

Insects are arthropods

Insects belong to a group of invertebrates called **arthropods**. Arthropods have hard coverings called **exoskeletons** on their bodies. An insect's exoskeleton covers its entire body. It even covers its legs and its head!

*There are thousands of different **species**, or types, of insects. This praying mantis is an insect.*

Body talk

An insect's body has three main sections—a head, a **thorax**, and an **abdomen**. The insect has eyes, **mouthparts**, and two **antennae** on its head. The insect's antennae are like feelers. The insect has six legs attached to its thorax. Some insects have wings. The wings are also attached to the thorax. The insect's **organs** are inside its abdomen.

dragonfly

Insects such as dragonflies have two pairs of wings. Other insects have only one pair of wings. Some insects have no wings at all.

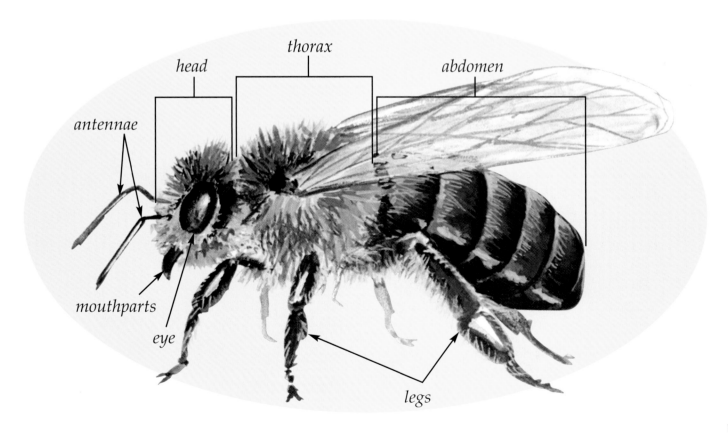

head

thorax

abdomen

antennae

mouthparts

eye

legs

5

where do insects live?

Insects live almost everywhere in the world. Most insects live in warm, moist **habitats**. A habitat is the natural place where an animal lives. Some insect habitats are swamps, **rain forests**, and soil. Habitats provide insects with the water, food, and the temperatures that insects need to stay alive.

These leaf-cutter ants live in a rain forest.

Finding space

Many insects have homes in their habitats. Some insect homes are simply spaces that insects find between rocks or plants. Other insects build their homes.

Happy homes

Different species of insects build homes of different sizes and shapes. Some insects dig **burrows**. A burrow is a tunnel that is dug into the ground or a hole in a tree. Other insect homes, such as the **hive** on the right, are more difficult to build. Hive-building insects live in large groups inside their homes.

This beetle is about to crawl into its burrow. The burrow will keep the beetle warm and safe.

7

Home sweet home

Insects use their homes in many ways. For example, they hide in their homes to avoid **predators**. Predators are animals that hunt and eat other animals. Many insects also use their homes to shelter them from bad weather. Insects that live in hot places go into their homes to cool their bodies. Insects that live in cold places may warm their bodies in their homes.

This wasp hides in its home from predators such as birds.

The nursery

Some insects use their homes as safe places to lay their eggs and raise their young. Most insects hatch from eggs. After hatching, many young insects go through a set of **stages**, or changes, as they grow. These stages are called **metamorphosis**. The four stages of a ladybug's metamorphosis are shown on the right.

Safe changes

As insects go through metamorphosis, many cannot protect themselves from harsh weather and from predators. The growing insects are safe from harm inside their homes, however.

A ladybug starts its life inside an egg.

*After hatching, the ladybug is a **larva**.*

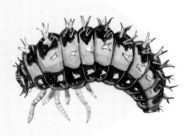

*During the third stage of metamorphosis, the ladybug is a **pupa**.*

The ladybug has completed metamorphosis when it is an adult.

9

Holes for homes

Some insects dig burrows into the ground. Others dig burrows into logs or trees. Most insects that dig burrows are **solitary** insects. Solitary insects live alone. Certain species of beetles, crickets, and wasps live in burrows.

A tight squeeze

A burrow's tunnel is just wide enough for the insect to squeeze through. This tight fit helps keep larger animals out of the burrow.

This solitary bee is about to enter its burrow. Like most insect burrows, this burrow is a small hole in the ground that is hard for other animals spot.

10

Back to the burrow

Some insects bring food back to their burrows. When a wood wasp kills an insect, for example, it brings the **prey** to its burrow. Prey are animals that predators hunt and eat. Once the wasp is inside its burrow, it eats the prey.

Did you know?
Some insects live in places that have cold winters. These insects survive cold weather by staying inside their warm burrows.

This wood wasp is carrying prey back to its burrow.

Homes in wood

Many insects make their homes in plants, especially trees. Some insects also eat plants, so their homes provide them with both shelter and food!

Chewing out

Some insects, including carpenter bees, have strong jaws that can cut through hard tree bark and wood. Carpenter bees chew through wood to make **chambers**, or rooms, in which they will live. Other insects chew through rotten logs. Rotten wood is soft and easy for some insects to chew.

*Carpenter bees do not eat the wood they chew. They eat **pollen** and drink **nectar** from flowers. This carpenter bee has pollen on its back.*

Slide inside

Insects that live in wood often have bodies that are able to slip under the bark of logs or squeeze through small cracks in wood. The beetle larva shown below has a thin body. The insect wiggles easily in and out of the cracks in a rotten log.

Did you know?

Some insects do not live in plants, but they lay their eggs in plants. Plants are often safe spots for young insects to grow. Many female solitary insects have long, thin body parts called **ovipositors**. The insects use their ovipositors to lay eggs in hard-to-reach areas inside trees or plant stems.

This ichneumon wasp has a long ovipositor that can drill deep into bark.

Living large

Some insects are **social** insects. Social insects live in large groups called **colonies**. Some colonies have over one million insects! Ants, honeybees, termites, and some species of wasps are social insects.

Working together

Insects that live in colonies work together to fight off predators. They also work together to build homes with many rooms. Young insects live in some of the rooms. Other rooms are used for storing food. There are even rooms for garbage!

This colony of ants is working together in their home.

A job for each insect

Each insect in a colony belongs to a **caste**, or group. Each caste has jobs that help the colony survive. Honeybee castes and their jobs are described below.

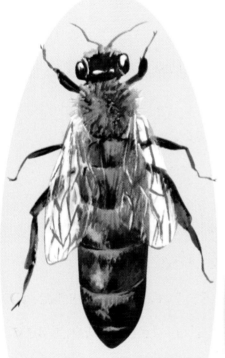

The **queen** is the leader of her colony. She lays thousands of eggs. Young honeybees hatch from the eggs.

A male honeybee is called a **drone**. His job is to **mate** with the queen honeybee.

A **worker** is a female honeybee. A worker builds, repairs, and protects the home. She also gathers food for the other insects in her colony.

Paper homes

Some wasps build hives under ground. Others build hives that hang from trees. The hive shown above is hanging from a tree.

Hive wasps such as yellow jackets and paper wasps are social insects. They live in hives. A colony of hive wasps is made up of workers, drones, and a queen. The worker wasps build and repair the colony's hive.

Busy builders

To build a hive, worker wasps chew wood and mix it with their **saliva**. The saliva softens the chewed wood into **pulp**. The workers use their mouthparts and legs to shape the pulp into small **cells**. Each cell has a **hexagonal**, or six-sided, shape. This shape makes the cells strong. A wall of cells is called a **comb**.

These wasps are making cells for their hive.

Wrap it up!

Once the combs are shaped, the pulp hardens into a paper-like material. The workers then build thin coverings, called **envelopes**, around the combs. The envelopes keep cold air out of the hive. If the hive is damaged, workers make more pulp and repair any holes.

Worker wasps make sure there are no holes in their hive.

Hive alive!

Some species of social bees live together in hives. The cells in honeybee hives are made of **beeswax**. Beeswax is a substance that worker bees make inside their bodies. Beeswax comes out of their bodies in flakes. The bees use their their legs and mouthparts to soften the flakes of wax. Then they shape the wax into cells.

*A worker honeybee makes a sticky, gluelike liquid called **resin** inside its body. The worker uses resin to repair cells and to hold together parts of the hive.*

Honeybee cells

Different cells in a honeybee hive are used for different purposes. Many cells contain eggs. The queen lays as many as 1,000 eggs a day! She lays one egg in each cell. Some cells contain larvae. In another part of the hive, the cells contain food such as nectar and honey.

Did you know?
Honeybees make honey by gathering nectar from flowers and storing it in cells. Over time, the stored nectar changes into honey. Adult honeybees and honeybee larvae eat the honey.

Bees often cover cells with caps made of wax. Some of the cells in this hive have wax caps.

Nifty nests

Most ants build homes on or under the ground. Ant homes are called **nests**. Ant nests are full of winding tunnels. They also have many rooms. Ants use their jaws and legs to dig tunnels and move dirt. As they make their nests, ants create **anthills**. Anthills are piles of dirt or sand outside the nests. Some anthills are tiny bumps on the ground. Others can be six feet (1.8 m) tall!

An ant nest is home to a colony of ants. The ant colony is made up of workers, males, and a queen.

Down on the farm

Many ants have farms in their homes! They use one room in the nest to grow **fungi** to eat. To grow fungi, worker ants gather bits of leaves and bring them back to the nest. Another group of workers then takes the leaves to the farm. At the farm, the workers add ant waste to the leaves. The waste causes fungi to grow.

These leaf-cutter ants are farmers. They are carrying bits of leaves back to their nest.

Termite builders

A termite colony is made up of workers, **soldiers**, a **king**, and a queen. Worker termites have many of the same jobs as those of worker honeybees. Soldier termites guard the colony. The king is the only termite that mates with the queen.

Termite homes

Some termites build nests made of sticks and soil in trees. Other termites build their homes under the ground or in wood. The termites dig into dirt or trees and make tunnels and rooms. Termites that live in wood are able to eat and **digest** wood.

Termites do not like sunlight. They avoid sunlight by staying inside their homes.

Termite mounds

Some termites build huge homes called **mounds**. The mounds are made of a mixture of soil, saliva, and termite waste. Some termite mounds are over 30 feet (9 m) high! More than one million termites may live inside one mound. Worker termites work constantly to clean and repair their home.

Did you know?
Most species of insects live for only a few days or a few weeks. Worker and soldier termites often live for three to five years, however. A termite colony's king and queen can live for over fifteen years! Their strong, safe homes protect the termites throughout their long lives.

Giant termite mounds are very strong. A person would need a hammer to break down a termite mound!

Dirt City

A **termite mound** is like a city. Underneath the huge mound are tunnels and **galleries**, or long rooms. Most of the termites live there. The main galleries are found about ten feet (3 m) below the ground. The gallery where the queen and king termites live is in the middle of the mound. It is called the **royal chamber**.

*A queen termite, shown left, never leaves the royal chamber. Worker termites bring her food and water. Other workers gather her eggs and move them to **nursery galleries**, where young termites are raised.*

Food and water

Many of the tunnels in a termite mound lead out of the mound, so workers can leave to gather food. Termites eat wood, seeds, **lichens**, and other plants. They use some of the food to grow fungi in farms. Termite farms are similar to ant farms. The deepest tunnels in a termite mound lead down to **ground water**, or water found deep in the ground. The termites need the ground water to survive.

Did you know?

A termite mound is air-conditioned! The mound has **vents**, or openings, that allow hot air to escape from the mound. Workers keep their home at a comfortable temperature by either removing or adding soil to the vents.

A soldier termite has large, powerful jaws. Soldiers guard the entrances to the mounds.

Moving in

Some species of insects make **temporary** homes as they move from place to place. Army ants make temporary homes. Army ants are almost always on the move. When they need to rest, they stop and make a nest wherever they are. The nest is called a **bivouac**. Army ants make a bivouac by clinging to one another and forming a ball with their bodies. The queen, the eggs, and the larvae are safe inside the bivouac.

Unwelcome guests

Some insect species live in homes built by other insects. A few of these species are allowed into the nests, but others are not! Some ant colonies welcome certain beetles into their homes because the beetles feed and protect the ants. The ants do not welcome other queen ants, however. Once a queen ant is inside a nest, she has the old queen killed! She then becomes the new queen of the colony.

Parasitic wasps use the bodies of other animals as their nurseries! They use their stingers to lay eggs on the bodies of moth caterpillars. Wasp larvae hatch from the eggs and live on the caterpillars. The larvae slowly eat the caterpillars until they die. This caterpillar was a meal for dozens of wasp larvae.

Helpful homes

Some insect homes are helpful to other animals and people. For example, people and animals eat honey from honeybee hives. **Beekeepers** are people who collect the honey from the hives and provide honeybees with places to live.

Honeybees eat some of the honey they make in their hives. A beekeeper collects the extra honey.

Did you know?
By building nests in soil, insects help plants grow. Ant nests are made up of many winding tunnels. The tunnels allow air to travel down into the soil. When there is air in the soil, the soil is healthy and plants have plenty of **oxygen**. Oxygen is a gas in the air that people, animals, and plants need to breathe. Plants need oxygen to grow and survive.

Mounds of fun

Play this game to see how it feels to be a busy termite. Be the first worker termite to journey through the mound and bring food and water to your king and queen.

Needed to play
game pieces
one die

How to play
To begin, place your game piece on the "start" space. Roll the die and move your piece through the termite mound, following the directions as you go. The first worker termite to journey through the mound and bring food and water to the king and queen wins!

To make a bigger game, you can draw this game onto a piece of bristol board. If you like, you can add even more termite challenges.

VENTS

The nest is too hot. Move ahead 4 spaces to clear the vents.

The vents need to be closed. Move back 1 space.

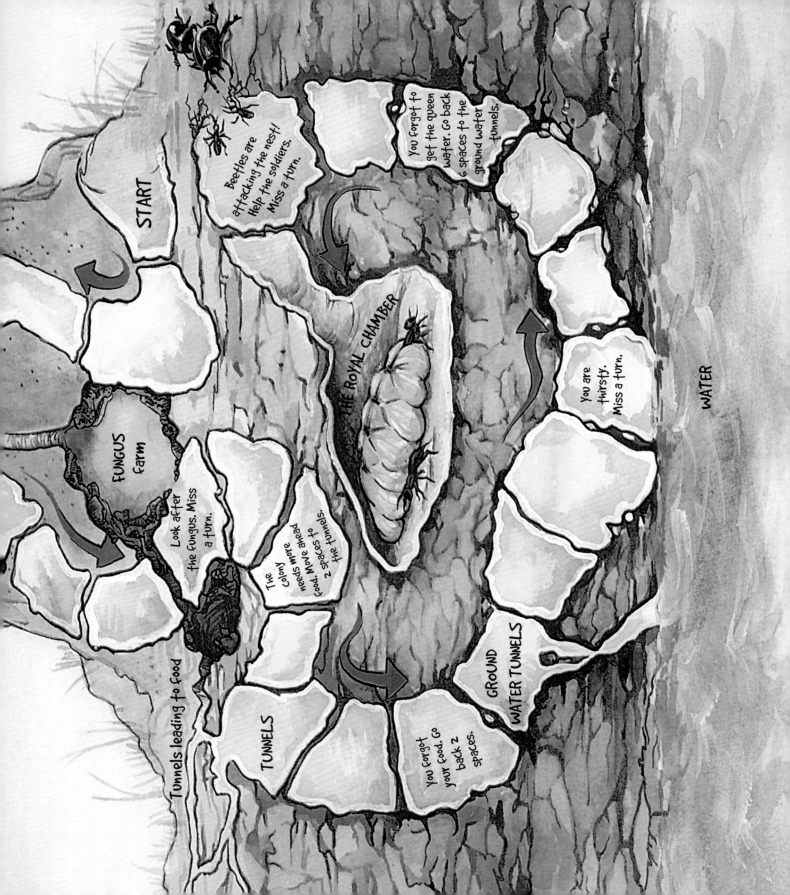

Glossary

Note: Boldfaced words that are defined in the text may not appear in the glossary.

cell A six-sided space inside a hive

digest To break down food in the stomach

fungi Plantlike living things that feed on living and dead things

hive The place where bees and wasps live

lichen A type of plant that grows on rocks, walls, or trees

mate To join together to make babies

nectar A sweet liquid found in flowers

organ A body part, such as the heart, that does an important job

pollen A powdery substance that plants make

pulp A soft, wet clump of wood

rain forest A forest that receives over 80 inches (203 cm) of rain each year

saliva A clear liquid found in an animal's mouth

temporary Describing something that is used for a short time

Index

1 2 3 4 5 6 7 8 9 0 Printed in the U.S.A. 5 4 3 2 1 0 9 8 7 6